BEST
SALTY
SWEET
SNACKS

BEST
SALTY
SWEET
SNACKS

GOOEY, CHEWY, CRUNCHY
TREATS FOR EVERY CRAVING

MONICA SWEENEY

THE COUNTRYMAN PRESS

A DIVISION OF W. W. NORTON & COMPANY

INDEPENDENT PUBLISHERS SINCE 1923

For information about permission to reproduce selections from this book, write to Permissions, The Countryman Press, 500 Fifth Avenue, New York, NY 10110

For information about special discounts for bulk purchases, please contact W. W. Norton Special Sales at specialsales@wwnorton.com or 800-233-4830

The Countryman Press
www.countrymanpress.com

A division of W. W. Norton & Company, Inc.,
500 Fifth Avenue, New York, NY 10110
www.wwnorton.com

978-1-58157-390-9 (pbk.)

10 9 8 7 6 5 4 3 2 1

FOR SHIRLEY

BEST SALTY SWEET SNACKS
CONTENTS

Chapter Three: Crunchy Snacks / 65

Chapter Four: Chocolaty Snacks / 85

Chapter Five: Nutty Snacks / 101

Introduction

When a craving hits, it's usually a strong urge for something salty or something sweet, but why should anyone be forced to choose? Your taste buds deserve better. Thankfully, there is an elite category of scrumptious treats that take snack time satisfaction to a whole new level. In the *Best Salty Sweet Snacks* cookbook, you'll find dozens of creative and delicious recipes to suit all of your between-meal cravings.

These quick and easy snacks are guaranteed to add a touch of fun to an otherwise regular day or the usual gathering of friends and family. That's because they all rely on a fail-safe formula for snack-time success: When you dare to pair salty and sweet ingredients, you are rewarded with dynamic and delicious food.

Each chapter provides a new texture or flavor experience. Start at Chapter One and choose from a gooey assortment of snacks drizzled with caramel and oozing with chocolate and marshmallow. When you're in the mood for something that works great as an appetizer, flip to Chapter Two and its savory meats cooked in sweet maple syrup or its fried vegetables paired with tangy dressings. Chapter Three offers even more snacks, all of which are made crunchy with ingredients like salty potato chip pieces, fluffs of popcorn, and crisp cereals. Still hungry? The chocolate lover in you will be drawn to the unique combinations in Chapter Four. Finish off your tour of all things snack-able and delicious with Chapter Five's nut-centric mix of candied almonds, cheesy pecans, and peanut-laden caramel.

With this collection of satisfying recipes, you are ready to turn game day into mouth-watering, bite-sized-treats day and movie night into a can't-eat-just-one celebration. These yummy recipes are designed with your busy life in mind and incorporate store-bought ingredients and helpful shortcuts whenever possible. Everyone, from rookie chefs to kitchen gurus, will have a blast preparing and sharing their new favorite salty-sweet snacks.

CHAPTER ONE

GOOEY SNACKS

Salted Caramel Pecan Tarts

Serve these scrumptious tarts at your next social gathering and they will instantly draw a crowd. From the flaky crust to the creamy caramel filling packed with crunchy salted nuts, this dessert is designed to satisfy a whole slew of cravings at once.

Yield: 12 mini tarts

2 ready-made pie crusts

3 large eggs

⅔ cup sugar

1 (12.25-ounce) jar caramel topping

¼ cup butter, melted

1½ cups salted pecan halves

Preheat oven to 350°F. Roll out pie crusts and use a glass or a 4-inch round cutter to cut 6 circles of dough from each crust. Press dough circles gently into a greased muffin tin. In a medium bowl, beat eggs. Add sugar, stirring until blended. Stir in caramel, melted butter, and pecan halves. Pour filling into each miniature crust. Bake for 45 minutes. Remove from oven and allow to cool before serving.

Chocolate Hazelnut Tarts with Sea Salt & Crushed Hazelnuts

When you're looking for a delicious, gooey chocolate hazelnut snack that doesn't require a lot of ingredients, these sea-salted Nutella tarts are the answer. Ready-made pie crusts and a jar of hazelnut spread make them fast and easy to prepare. Add a pinch of sea salt and some crunchy hazelnuts for topping and you have the perfect miniature treat.

Yield: 12 mini tarts

CRUST:

2 ready-made pie crusts

FILLING:

2 cups Cool Whip

1 cup Nutella or store-brand chocolate/hazelnut spread

TOPPING:

½ cup chopped hazelnuts

1 tablespoon coarse sea salt

Preheat oven to 350°F. Roll out pie crusts and use a glass or a 4-inch round cutter to cut 6 circles of dough from each crust. Press dough circles gently into greased muffin tin. Bake tart crusts for 20 minutes using pie weights. Remove weights and cook for 10 more minutes or until edges are golden brown. In a medium bowl, mix together Cool Whip and Nutella until combined. Scoop the chocolate hazelnut filling into each mini pie crust. Sprinkle with crushed hazelnuts and salt, then serve.

Salted Caramel Cupcakes

These cupcakes allow the taste of salty-sweet caramel to take center stage. With creamy, homemade caramel frosting and indulgent add-ons like sea salt and chocolate chips, these cupcakes are rich with flavor. To add another dimension of caramel, you could fill these with squeezable caramel sauce (use a melon baller to carve a hole in the top of each cupcake) after they have cooled.

Yield: 12 cupcakes

1 box yellow cake mix, plus required box ingredients

CARAMEL BUTTERCREAM FROSTING:

1½ cups unsalted butter, cubed

4 ounces cream cheese, cubed

1 cup caramel sauce, plus extra for drizzling

3 cups confectioners' sugar

TOPPING:

1 teaspoon sea salt

¼ cup miniature chocolate chips (for sprinkling)

Caramel sauce (for drizzling)

Prepare cupcakes according to directions on the box. Allow to cool. With an electric mixer on low, beat the cubed butter until smooth. Add in the cream cheese and caramel sauce and beat until fully combined. Mix in the confectioners' sugar, 1 cup at a time. Frost cupcakes with caramel frosting and sprinkle each cupcake with sea salt, chocolate chips, and a drizzle of caramel if desired before serving.

Maple Walnut
Mini Cheesecakes

These adorable cakes make the perfect afternoon or evening treat, and are made even more flavorful with a generous maple syrup topping. Top with salted almonds, pecans, or walnuts and you've got a delicious reason to pause for a snack break.

Yield: 10 cheesecakes

1 (8-ounce) package cream cheese, softened

⅓ cup real maple syrup, plus 2 tablespoons for topping

1 teaspoon vanilla

1 egg

2 tablespoons all-purpose flour

¼ cup salted nuts

Preheat oven to 325°F. In a large mixing bowl, beat cream cheese until fluffy, gradually mixing in maple syrup and vanilla until smooth. Add in egg and flour and mix until combined. Pour filling into a greased cupcake tin. Bake for about 15 minutes. Drizzle with syrup, cover, and refrigerate for 1 to 2 hours. Sprinkle with nuts before serving.

Caramel Nut
Apple Dippers

A caramel apple on a stick is the perfect snack for kids who don't mind getting messy. This slightly more grown-up version of caramel apples features crunchy apple slices that are perfectly sized, easy to customize, and bring together salty chopped nuts and gooey sweet caramel. When serving these at a gathering, spear each slice with a toothpick to guarantee mess-free eating. I use Granny Smith apples in this recipe because of their bold, tart flavor, but you can use any apple that you like.

Yield: 4 servings

20 square caramel candies

1½ tablespoons whipping cream

¼ teaspoon sea salt

2 to 3 apples, sliced

1 cup salted nuts, finely chopped

In a microwave-safe bowl at 30-second intervals, melt caramels, whipping cream, and salt together until smooth. Stir to blend completely. Dry apple slices with a paper towel and dip each slice into the caramel mixture until about half the apple is submerged. Roll dipped slices in salted nuts and place on wax paper to set. Serve immediately.

Dark Chocolate Pretzel Brownies

These rich chocolate brownies are a little bite of heaven, especially if they're eaten when still warm from the oven. Start with your favorite brownie box mix and add chocolate-covered pretzels (plain pretzels will lose their crunch) to create a simple salty-sweet snack that's fresh-baked perfection.

Yield: 16 servings

1 box dark chocolate brownie mix

½ cup vegetable oil

¼ cup water

2 eggs

1 cup chocolate-covered pretzel pieces (dark, white, or milk chocolate)

Preheat oven to 350°F. Whisk brownie mix, vegetable oil, water, and eggs together in a large bowl. Fold in pretzel pieces. Pour batter into lightly greased 13 x 9-inch baking dish. Bake for 25 to 30 minutes or until toothpick comes out clean. Allow to cool before slicing into squares and serving.

Salted Butterscotch Fudge

Caramel is not the only flavor that is greatly enhanced by a touch of salt. Butter-scotch also makes a delightfully smooth and creamy starting point for many of the best salted snacks. Follow this simple fudge recipe for a platter of tasty morsels that will make you swoon with every bite. When you want a satisfying crunch, add a cup of almonds or pecans to this recipe.

Yield: 12 to 15 servings

3 cups butterscotch chips

1 tablespoon butter

1 (14-ounce) can sweetened condensed milk

1 teaspoon almond extract

½ teaspoon sea salt

Line a 9 x 9-inch baking pan with foil and coat in cooking spray. In a medium saucepan over medium heat, add butterscotch chips, butter, and sweetened condensed milk. Stir until combined and fully melted. Remove from heat and stir in almond extract. Pour fudge into baking pan. Immediately sprinkle with sea salt. Refrigerate until firm, about 2 to 3 hours.

Candy Shop Marshmallow Treats

Rice Krispies Treats get a salty-sweet makeover when you add in candy shop indulgences like caramel sauce, peanuts, chocolate, and your all-time favorite candy bar! I like to crumble little pieces of Snickers over my finished treats, but Almond Joys, Reese's Peanut Butter Cups, and Kit Kats are also excellent additions to this sinfully rich dessert.

Yield: 12 servings

3 tablespoons butter

1 (10-ounce) bag marshmallows

6 cups Rice Krispies cereal

¼ cup caramel sauce

½ cup salted peanuts, crushed

½ cup Snickers or other candy bar, broken into small pieces

1 cup chocolate syrup or semisweet chocolate chips, melted

Melt butter in large saucepot over low heat. Stir in marshmallows and keep stirring until melted. Add Rice Krispies cereal and coat until stringy with marshmallow. Mix in caramel sauce, peanuts, and candy bar pieces. Empty mixture into 13 x 9-inch greased baking pan and use a piece of wax paper to gently press into an even layer. Cool for 10 minutes. Drizzle chocolate syrup over the Krispies layer. Allow to set 30 minutes in refrigerator before serving.

Chocolate Walnut Pie

This classic pie is both gooey and nutty, thanks to the rich chocolate pudding filling and the crunchy walnuts whirled inside. It's unbelievably fast and easy to make, so it's perfect when you have an urgent craving that needs a quick solution. Top this treat with gobs of fluffy whipped topping and you're sure to want a second helping.

Yield: 8 servings

1 ready-made pie crust

2 (3.9-ounce) boxes instant chocolate pudding mix

4 cups cold milk

1 cup walnut pieces

Bake pie crust as directed. Meanwhile, whisk pudding mix and milk together for 2 minutes until it thickens into pudding. Fold in walnuts. Pour into baked, cooled pie shell and refrigerate for 1 to 2 hours before serving.

Caramel Peanut Cookies

These easy-to-make peanut butter cookies are a crowd-pleasing choice for any gathering. With a gooey pool of caramel topping in the center and a sprinkling of crushed peanuts instead of the traditional pecans, there's a lot to like about these reinvented sandies.

Yield: 16 cookies

1 egg

1 cup peanut butter (creamy or crunchy—your preference)

1 cup sugar

TOPPING:

⅓ cup caramel sauce

½ cup peanuts, crushed

Preheat oven to 350°F. In a large mixing bowl, mix together egg, peanut butter, and sugar. Drop spoonfuls onto a cookie sheet an inch apart and flatten dough into discs using the back of a spoon. Gently press thumbs into centers of cookies. Bake for 10 to 12 minutes. Allow to cool before filling centers with a teaspoonful of caramel sauce and adding a sprinkling of crushed peanuts.

CHAPTER TWO

SAVORY SNACKS

Pineapple Mini Pizzas

For game-time snacking, these little Hawaiian pizzas can't be beat. Ham and pineapple are the perfect duo, especially when they are immersed in zesty pizza sauce and sprinkled with cheese. If you can't find small pre-made pizza crusts at the store, you can use refrigerated pizza dough and prep it before baking.

Yield: 8 servings

¼ cup pizza sauce

2 (8-inch) premade pizza crusts

2 cups shredded mozzarella cheese

1 (8-ounce) can pineapple tidbits, drained

½ cup deli ham pieces

Heat oven to 425°F. Spread pizza sauce onto dough. Top with cheeses, pineapple, and ham. Place on pizza stone or ungreased baking sheet and bake for 10 minutes or until cheese is melted and crust is golden brown.

Chili-Brown Sugar Roasted Chickpeas

Put a bowlful of these savory chickpeas on the table and people will instinctively gravitate to them. Pop them in your mouth and you'll enjoy a whole bouquet of flavors from spicy to salty to sweet. Adjust the cayenne pepper to take them from mild to fiery.

Yield: 4 to 6 servings

2 (14-ounce) cans chickpeas

2 tablespoons plus 1 teaspoon olive oil, divided

1 teaspoon salt, divided

2 tablespoons (packed) brown sugar

¼ to ½ teaspoon cayenne pepper

Preheat oven to 350°F. Rinse and drain chickpeas. Pour them into a bowl and dab them gently with a paper towel to dry. Add 2 tablespoons olive oil and ½ teaspoon salt to bowl and toss chickpeas until covered in oil and salt. Arrange in a single layer on a baking sheet. Roast for 40 to 50 minutes or until chickpeas are golden brown and crisp.

Meanwhile, combine brown sugar, 1 teaspoon olive oil, cayenne pepper, and remaining salt in a medium bowl. Pour the roasted chickpeas into the bowl and toss with the brown sugar mixture. Allow to cool before serving.

Ham & Cheese Pretzel Bites with Maple Syrup Mustard Dip

This shortcut recipe uses ready-to-bake dinner rolls as the starting ingredient. Ham and cheese slices are stuffed inside and the rolls are lightly salted. Consider using swiss cheese instead of cheddar if you prefer a milder flavor. Don't forget to make extra so you can sample this savory sauce with french fries, chicken fingers, and fresh veggies.

Yield: 6 to 8 servings

PRETZEL ROLLS:

12 frozen dinner rolls, thawed

6 slices cheddar cheese, quartered

5 slices deli ham, cut into 1½-inch squares

1 egg, slightly beaten

1 teaspoon water

1 to 2 teaspoons coarse sea salt

DIP:

½ cup Dijon mustard

¼ cup real maple syrup

Preheat oven to 350°F. Flatten thawed rolls and place a few squares of cheese and several ham squares in center. Fold edges of dough inward and seal dough around cheese, pinching edges tightly. Repeat with remaining rolls. Place onto a well-greased baking sheet. Brush each roll with a mixture of beaten egg and water. Sprinkle with coarse salt. Bake for 10 to 15 minutes or until golden brown.

Combine dip ingredients and serve alongside pretzel bites.

Apple Baked Brie

Sweet fruits and salty cheese are a culinary match made in heaven. Try this simple apple tart recipe that bakes a pinwheel of apple slices on top of a warm, bubbling layer of baked Brie. This is a fantastic comfort-food snack to serve at any gathering.

Yield: 10 servings

1 tablespoon butter

2 firm apples (Granny Smiths work well), cored and sliced thinly

½ cup packed brown sugar

1 tablespoon apple juice

1 teaspoon ground cinnamon

1 (8-ounce) round Brie cheese

Heat oven to 350°F. In a small frying pan, melt butter over low heat. Add apple slices, brown sugar, apple juice, and ground cinnamon. Cook, stirring frequently, until apples are softened. Place Brie round in an ungreased 9-inch pie plate or baking dish. Spoon softened apple slices onto Brie. Bake 15 to 20 minutes or until cheese is warmed through. Serve warm.

Spiced Sweet Potato Fries

Freshly baked sweet potato fries get even more exciting when you add in a variety of palate-pleasing spices like fiery cayenne, aromatic cumin, and hints of garlic and onion. The secret to a crispy batch of glistening, golden fries is soaking the potato strips in a bowl of cold water for an hour or so before baking. This reduces the starch levels and eliminates any sogginess.

Yield: 4 to 6 servings

½ tablespoon chili powder

½ tablespoon ground cumin

½ teaspoon onion powder

½ teaspoon garlic powder

¼ to ½ teaspoon cayenne pepper

2 medium sweet potatoes, washed and cut into ¼-inch strips

2 tablespoons olive oil

¼ teaspoon salt

Preheat oven to 450°F. In a large bowl, combine chili powder, cumin, onion powder, garlic powder, and cayenne. Add the sweet potato fries to the bowl and toss to coat the fries with seasoning. Add olive oil and toss again. Bake for 15 minutes on a foil-lined baking sheet, checking frequently to prevent burning. Season with salt before serving.

Fried Pickle Chips with Sweet Horseradish Dipping Sauce

Most of us have been lucky enough to sample breaded pickle chips like these at our local pubs and restaurants, and nearly everyone who tries them loves them. Fortunately, they're surprisingly easy to make from scratch. With a few simple ingredients you can bread and fry these crunchy little slices of heaven for all to enjoy.

Yield: 8 to 10 servings

FRIED PICKLE CHIPS:

2 cups vegetable oil

1 (32-ounce) jar dill pickle slices, drained

1 cup flour

2 eggs, beaten

1½ cups panko bread crumbs

1 teaspoon black pepper

¼ teaspoon garlic powder

½ teaspoon cayenne pepper

SWEET HORSERADISH DIPPING SAUCE:

1 (8-ounce) jar mayonnaise

4 tablespoons honey mustard sauce

1 tablespoon horseradish sauce

Splash of orange juice

Heat the oil in a large skillet over medium heat. Use paper towels to lay out the pickle slices and gently pat them dry. Place flour in a shallow bowl suitable for dipping. Place eggs in a second shallow bowl. Mix together the remaining four ingredients and place in a third shallow bowl. Dip pickles in flour, eggs, then breadcrumbs and fry in batches until golden brown on both sides. Allow to cool.

To prepare the sauce, simply mix together the first three ingredients and add orange juice until the sauce is the desired thickness for dipping. Cover and chill for 3 hours.

Sweet & Fiery Molasses Meatballs

For a cocktail meatball that runs the gamut in terms of flavor, try this recipe for Sweet & Fiery Molasses Meatballs. These stovetop meatballs are dripping with brown sugar and molasses. Chili powder and cayenne pepper add a layer of heat to every bite.

Yield: 8 to 10 servings

½ cup water

½ cup molasses

¼ cup brown sugar

1 teaspoon garlic powder

1 teaspoon chili powder

1 teaspoon ground ginger

¼ teaspoon cayenne pepper

2 pounds frozen cooked meatballs

Thin pretzel sticks (optional)

In a large saucepan on high heat, bring the water to a boil. Add molasses, brown sugar, garlic powder, chili powder, ginger, and cayenne. Stir until combined. Add in meatballs and continue to stir, reducing the heat to medium-low. Simmer for 15 to 20 minutes or until sauce thickens. Serve warm. Spear each meatball with a pretzel stick, if desired, when serving.

Honey-Mustard Bacon Rods

These bacon-wrapped pretzel rods are the best snack-on-a-stick out there. They reign supreme in terms of salty-sweet flavor power and grab-and-go convenience. This makes them ideal as a party snack or a fun appetizer for teenagers who can hardly wait for dinner to be ready.

Yield: 4 servings

1 pound regular-sliced bacon (not thick)

½ cup honey

½ cup Dijon mustard

Dash of cayenne pepper

12 pretzel rods

Preheat the oven to 350°F. Spread the bacon slices out on a lined baking sheet. Combine the honey and Dijon in a small bowl and brush the honey-mustard glaze onto the bacon strips. Sprinkle on the cayenne. Bake the bacon for 6 to 7 minutes, then remove from oven and let cool. Curl one strip of bacon around a pretzel rod and place the rod on the baking sheet with the end of the bacon tucked under. Do the same for the remaining pretzel rods. Bake for 5 to 7 more minutes. Remove from oven and allow to cool slightly before serving.

Candied Bacon Strips

Just when you thought bacon couldn't get any better, this recipe comes along and makes you literally eat your words. The maple syrup and brown sugar coating turns regular bacon into pure candied bliss. Throw in a kick of cayenne and you have an irresistible snack for game day or any day.

Yield: 4 servings

¼ cup brown sugar

2 tablespoons maple syrup

Dash of cayenne pepper

8 thick slices bacon

Preheat oven to 350°F. Mix together brown sugar, syrup, and cayenne pepper in a large bowl. Place bacon slices in bowl one at a time and coat with sugar mixture. Arrange slices on a wire rack over a baking pan coated with tinfoil. Bake for 20 minutes. Flip bacon and continue to bake for about 10 more minutes or until the bacon is dark and crisp. Remove from oven and allow to cool before serving.

Peanut Butter
Bacon Cookies

Every snack attack deserves the kind of relief these indulgent cookies provide. It begins with a few generous scoops of rich, chunky peanut butter, but the salty bacon crumble makes for a magnificent finish. If you've ever imagined what would happen when these ingredients joined forces, you're about to find out.

Yield: 24 cookies

1 cup chunky peanut butter

½ cup plus 2 tablespoons sugar, divided

½ cup brown sugar

1 egg

1 teaspoon baking soda

½ teaspoon vanilla extract

8 slices bacon, cooked and crumbled

Preheat oven to 350°F. In a large bowl, mix together peanut butter, ½ cup sugar, and brown sugar. Mix in egg, baking soda, and vanilla extract, and beat until fully combined and smooth. Fold in bacon crumble. Form dough into small 1½-inch balls. Roll balls in remaining sugar to coat before placing on an ungreased cookie sheet. Bake for 10 minutes or until edges begin to brown. Cool for 10 to 15 minutes before serving.

Bacon Caramel
Walnut Brownies

This salty-sweet, freshly baked treat is easy to make when you want to spoil yourself with a treasure trove of flavors. Every fudgy bite offers a medley of crunchy walnuts, crisp bacon, and warm melted caramel.

Yield: 16 brownies

1 box brownie mix

2 eggs

¼ cup water

½ cup vegetable oil

6 slices bacon, cooked and crumbled

½ cup chopped walnuts

¼ cup caramel sauce

Preheat oven to 350°F. In a large bowl, mix together brownie mix, eggs, water, and oil. Fold in bacon crumble and walnuts. Pour into an 8 x 8-inch baking pan. Bake for 30 to 35 minutes. Allow brownies to cool for 15 to 20 minutes before drizzling with caramel sauce. Let cool before serving.

Maple-Glazed Chicken Wings

These wings make the perfect appetizer for the next big sporting event. Instead of brushing on the glaze before you bake these and allowing all the flavor to drip off during the cooking process, it's better to add the glaze after the wings are cooked. The flour helps the sweet maple coating stick to every nook and cranny, and the final result is rich with flavor.

Yield: 3 to 4 servings

3 pounds chicken wings

2 tablespoons flour

Dash of salt and pepper

¾ cup maple syrup

¼ cup Dijon mustard

2 teaspoons Worcestershire sauce

Dash of cayenne pepper

Preheat oven to 400°F. Place wings and flour in a resealable plastic bag and shake to coat wings with flour. Arrange wings on a lined baking sheet and bake for 30 to 40 minutes, or until juices run clear. Meanwhile, in a small bowl, mix together remaining ingredients until well blended. Remove cooked wings from oven. Coat with maple syrup glaze. Bake glazed wings for an additional 5 minutes.

Sweet & Sour Shrimp

When you want something different and exciting to rev up your day, try these Sweet & Sour Shrimp. The sauce also can be used as a marinade: Just place shrimp in a plastic resealable bag with the sweet and sour sauce, and allow the shrimp to soak in the juices for 2 hours or more. Serve these tangy treats on skewers, with pineapples and maraschino cherries serving as edible garnish.

Yield: 4 servings

1 cup orange juice

3 tablespoons rice vinegar

3 tablespoons brown sugar

2 tablespoons soy sauce

2 tablespoons cornstarch mixed with 4 tablespoons water

1 tablespoon olive oil

1 pound large shrimp, peeled and deveined

In a medium bowl, mix the first five ingredients until fully blended. Add olive oil to a wok or skillet and bring to medium-high heat. Add shrimp to skillet and cook until opaque, about 3 to 4 minutes. Add sauce mixture to skillet and toss to coat. Stir-fry for 3 to 4 minutes. Remove from stovetop and pierce Sweet & Sour Shrimp with skewers before serving.

Bacon-Wrapped Dates with Blue Cheese Stuffing

If you've ever tried bacon-wrapped dates, you know they're the perfect flavor trio: salty, savory, and sweet. When it comes to snack time, nothing is simpler and yummier than stuffing a ripe fruit with soft cheese and wrapping it all up in a piece of bacon. Serve several on a skewer or spear individual dates with a toothpick for one-at-a-time snacking.

Yield: 24 dates

24 dried, pitted dates

1 (4-ounce) container crumbled blue cheese

12 slices bacon, cut in half

1 tablespoon honey

Preheat oven to 400°F. Make a slit in the side of each date and stuff with about a teaspoon of blue cheese crumble. Wrap each half slice of bacon around a date so that the stuffing is completely covered. Place on a greased baking sheet with the ends of the bacon tucked under each date. Bake for about 20 minutes or until bacon is crispy. Drizzle with honey before serving.

Cherry Corn Bread

Sometimes a fluffy square of cornbread is just the thing for a book club gathering or a midmorning snack. This recipe makes a fairly sweet corn bread, so consider reducing the sugar to highlight the tartness of the cherries. Need a quick fix? You can make this savory snack at a moment's notice by replacing the first five ingredients with a box of corn muffin mix and reducing the milk to ⅓ cup.

Yield: 8 servings

1 cup cornmeal

1 cup all-purpose flour

¼ cup sugar

4 teaspoons baking powder

½ teaspoon salt

1 cup milk

1 large egg

⅓ cup vegetable oil

1 cup tart pitted cherries

Preheat oven to 400°F. In a large bowl, mix together cornmeal, flour, sugar, baking powder, and salt. In a medium bowl, whisk together milk, egg, and oil.

Add wet ingredients to dry ingredients and stir until just combined. Fold in the cherries. Pour into a greased 8 x 8-inch baking dish and bake for 20 to 25 minutes or until the top begins to brown.

CHAPTER THREE

CRUNCHY SNACKS

Rainbow Chex Mix

When you're craving a crunchy snack with a variety of fun flavors, try this sweet and salty Chex party mix. Rice cereal and pretzels get a flavor makeover when they're coated in white chocolate and dusted with cake mix for a sensational snacking experience.

Yield: 10 servings

1 cup white chocolate chips

¼ cup salted butter

3 tablespoons heavy cream

1 teaspoon almond extract

9 cups Rice Chex cereal

1 cup miniature pretzels or pretzel sticks (halved)

1 cup Funfetti cake mix

¼ cup confectioners' sugar

In a medium saucepan over low heat, stir together white chocolate chips, butter, and cream until melted. Remove from heat. Add almond extract and stir. Pour the cereal and pretzels into a large bowl. Pour melted chocolate mixture over cereal. Mix very gently. Add cake mix and confectioners' sugar and mix gently until evenly coated. Allow to cool before serving.

Potato Chip-Battered Onion Rings

These crunchy, potato chip–crusted onion rings will make you wonder why you don't add potato chips to everything you fry. Serve them with a sweet dipping sauce, like honey mustard, to accentuate their delicious, salty crumble.

Yield: 4 servings

1 egg

¼ cup vegetable oil

1 cup milk

1½ cups flour, divided

½ teaspoon salt

1 teaspoon baking powder

4 cups potato chips, crumbled

2 large sweet onions, sliced into ½-inch thick rings

Oil (for frying)

In a medium bowl, mix together egg, oil, and milk. Mix in 1 cup flour, salt, and baking powder. Place potato chip crumble in a large shallow bowl nearby. Add remaining ½ cup flour to a separate shallow bowl. Dip onion slices in flour, then egg batter, then potato chip crumbs. Fry in oil in batches over medium-high heat until golden brown and crispy on both sides.

Bacon Caramel Corn

Give your regular microwave popcorn a serious upgrade with this simple salty-sweet variation. In just a few minutes you can prepare the warm caramel coating and drizzle it generously over salty fluffs of corn and tender flakes of delicious bacon. You'll want to revel in this snack's magnificent blend of flavors again and again.

Yield: 8 servings

8 cups popped popcorn

¾ cup packed light brown sugar

6 tablespoons butter

3 tablespoons light corn syrup

½ teaspoon vanilla extract

½ teaspoon baking soda

½ cup cooked bacon pieces (or bacon bits)

Preheat oven to 300°F. Pour popcorn into a large bowl. In a medium saucepan over medium heat, add brown sugar, butter, and corn syrup. Stir until boiling. Boil for 4 minutes. Remove from heat. Mix in vanilla and baking soda. Fold in bacon. Pour over popcorn and stir to coat. Spread caramel popcorn out on prepared baking sheet and bake for 5 to 10 minutes, checking frequently to prevent burning.

Apple-Cinnamon
Pretzel Mix

This salty-sweet party mix is great for days when you'd rather not have to turn on the oven. Simply toss the ingredients together in a bowl and prepared to be wowed by the combination of apple pie seasonings, creamy white chocolate, and salty nuts and grains.

Yield: 8 to 10 servings

4 cups Apple Cinnamon Cheerios (or apple-cinnamon flavored cereal)

2 cups miniature pretzels

1 cup lightly salted almonds

1 cup raisins

½ cup white chocolate chips

In a large bowl, combine all ingredients and stir until evenly distributed.

Chocolate Marshmallow Popcorn Balls

Nothing brings out the kid in everyone like a giant popcorn ball, especially when it's stuck together with buttery marshmallows and melted chocolate. When you need a new treat for movie night, these sweet and crunchy popcorn balls are the perfect choice.

Yield: 10 servings

¼ cup butter or margarine

40 large marshmallows

½ teaspoon vanilla

¼ teaspoon salt

½ cup semisweet chocolate chips

12 cups popped salted popcorn

In a large saucepan over low heat, melt together butter, marshmallows, vanilla, and salt. Mix until well blended. Stir in chocolate chips, allowing them to melt almost completely. Place popcorn in a large mixing bowl. Drizzle with the marshmallow/chocolate mixture and stir gently to coat. Shape into 10 (3-inch) balls, using wax paper so the popcorn doesn't stick to your hands while you work. Allow to cool and serve.

Potato Stick Butterscotch Haystacks

These butterscotch haystacks have more to offer than just a fun shape and a beautiful golden color. Each bite is packed with creamy butterscotch and chunks of salty peanuts. Because these are so rich in flavor, you can easily portion them into miniature haystacks for bite-sized fun. If you can't find potato sticks at the store, use chow mein noodles as a substitute.

Yield: 16 to 20 servings

½ cup peanut butter (crunchy or creamy—your preference)

1 cup butterscotch chips

2 cups potato sticks

½ cup salted peanuts, chopped

Heat peanut butter in a saucepan over medium heat. Reduce heat to low and add butterscotch chips, stirring until almost melted. Remove pot from burner, adding in potato sticks a little at a time while stirring the mixture. Once combined, fold in peanuts. Portion small heaps onto wax paper with a fork. Allow to set for 1 hour before serving.

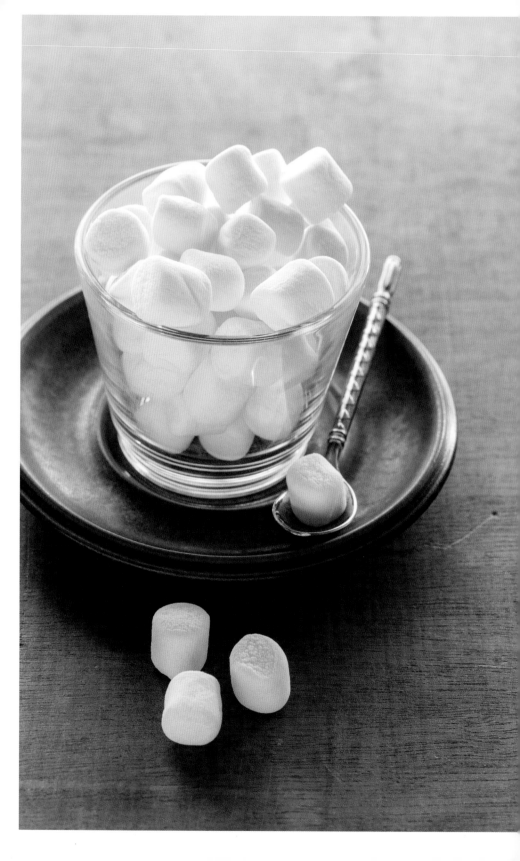

Marshmallow-Stuffed Snack Cones

There are dozens of creative ways to transform the popular instrument-shaped snack, the Bugle, into adorable bite-size treats. This marshmallow-stuffed version is one of my favorites. It takes a little time to stuff each Bugle, but the tiny, crunchy, bet-you-can't-eat-just-one results are worth the trouble. You might want to double the recipe because these are guaranteed to disappear fast.

Yield: 2 servings

$2\frac{2}{3}$ cups Bugles corn chip snacks

2 cups mini marshmallows

1 cup semisweet chocolate chips, melted

Rainbow sprinkles

Arrange Bugles on a wax-lined cookie sheet. Gently stuff each Bugle with a marshmallow. Dip the marshmallow end of the Bugle into a bowl of melted chocolate chips and top with rainbow sprinkles. Allow chocolate coating to harden before serving.

Oatmeal-Raisin Peanut Butter Cookies

Sometimes the favorites of yesterday deserve a space on today's snack plate. You can't improve upon a classic like oatmeal-raisin cookies, unless of course you combine it with the traditional peanut butter cookie. Together, these timeless cookies make an outstanding bite-size treat for any day of the week.

Yield: 24 cookies

½ cup butter, softened

¾ cup light brown sugar

¼ cup sugar

½ cup peanut butter (crunchy or creamy—your preference)

2 eggs

1 teaspoon vanilla extract

1 teaspoon baking soda

½ teaspoon salt

½ teaspoon cinnamon

1 cup all-purpose flour

1 cup old-fashioned rolled oats

¾ cup raisins

Preheat oven to 375°F. In a large bowl, cream together butter, both sugars, and peanut butter. Mix in eggs, vanilla, baking soda, salt, and cinnamon. Slowly stir in flour and oats. Fold in raisins. Drop spoonfuls of batter onto a greased baking sheet. Bake for 10 minutes or until golden brown.

Blueberry-Cream Cheese Walnut Bars

For pie lovers who crave an easy homemade snack, these Blueberry Cream Cheese Walnut Bars are unmatched. From the crumbly walnut-rich crust to the smooth, creamy cheesecake layer and the gooey blueberry topping, each square provides an adventure for your taste buds. When you need it fast, use a store-bought graham cracker pie crust and sprinkle the walnuts onto your finished bars.

Yield: 8 servings

CRUST:

1 cup graham cracker crumbs

¾ cup roasted, salted walnuts, finely chopped

¼ cup confectioners' sugar

⅓ cup butter, melted

TOPPING:

1 (8-ounce) package cream cheese

½ cup confectioners' sugar

1½ teaspoons vanilla

1 (8-ounce) container Cool Whip

1 can blueberry pie filling

In a medium bowl, mix together crust ingredients. Press firmly into the bottom of a greased 13 x 9-inch pan. Allow to set in freezer. In a separate bowl, mix together cream cheese, confectioners' sugar, vanilla, and Cool Whip. Spread onto chilled crust. Refrigerate for 1 to 2 hours. Spread on blueberry pie filling and chill in refrigerator before cutting into squares and serving.

CHAPTER FOUR

CHOCOLATY SNACKS

Gourmet Chocolate-Covered Pretzels

When you combine salty pretzels with thick, melted chocolate, the possibilities are truly endless. You can use white, milk, or dark chocolate—or even a little of each— to coat pretzels. This recipe works with pretzel sticks and traditional pretzels, large and small. Enjoy the freedom that comes with this foolproof recipe for a salty-sweet, bite-size snack. When you're in a festive mood, these little wonders can also be rolled in miniature chocolate chips or rainbow sprinkles.

Yield: 10 to 12 servings

1 cup semisweet chocolate chips

1 (15-ounce) bag pretzels

1 tablespoon sea salt

Melt chocolate chips in the microwave at 50-percent power in 20-second intervals or in a double boiler over medium-low heat until just about melted, then stir until smooth. Using tongs, dip each pretzel into the chocolate until completely coated. Lay coated pretzels on a wax paper–lined baking sheet and sprinkle with sea salt. Let the chocolate-covered pretzels harden before serving.

Toffee S'mores Chocolate Bark

Buttery toffee flavor is the perfect accent for this salty-sweet chocolate bark recipe. With a bottom layer of candied graham crackers and a topping of your favorite sweets all melted together, this is a treat to be enjoyed with pure abandon.

Yield: 15 servings

15 graham crackers

1 cup unsalted butter, cubed

1 cup packed light brown sugar

½ teaspoon pure vanilla extract

Pinch of sea salt

1 cup semisweet chocolate chips, melted

½ cup milk chocolate toffee squares, broken into small pieces

½ cup mini marshmallows

Preheat oven to 350°F. Line a baking sheet with aluminum foil and arrange graham cracker squares to cover the sheet. In a small saucepan, melt butter over low heat and mix in brown sugar until fully combined. Bring to a boil and cook for just a few minutes until the mixture thickens. Remove from heat. Stir in vanilla and salt. Pour over crackers. Bake crackers for 10 minutes or until bubbly but not burned. Remove the crackers from the oven and layer with melted chocolate chips, chocolate toffee bits, and mini marshmallows. Allow toppings to soften, then spread with a spatula over the top of the crackers to form an even layer. If needed, heat again in the oven until toppings melt enough to spread. Allow to set in refrigerator or freezer. Break apart and serve.

Chocolate-Covered Potato Chips

This recipe is so simple it practically makes itself. All you have to do is dip some of your favorite chips in a vat of smooth, milky chocolate, and you'll be rewarded with a sweet, crunchy potato treat that's popular with just about everyone. Try dipping just the bottom half of the chip into the chocolate to allow the salty to balance the sweet.

Yield: 8 servings

1¼ cups milk chocolate chips

4 cups potato chips

Melt chocolate chips in the microwave at 50-percent power in 20-second intervals or in a double boiler over medium-low heat. Check frequently and remove when almost fully melted. Stir chocolate until chips are fully melted and smooth. With a pair of tongs, grip each potato chip and dip it into the chocolate mixture until it is fully coated. Lay on a piece of wax paper until chocolate cools and sets, and serve.

Salted Chocolate Coconut Fudge

When you want a rich snack that's bursting with fudgy chocolate flavor, Salted Chocolate Coconut Fudge is just the thing. You'll love the texture that coconut adds, but there's nothing wrong with leaving it out so you can enjoy the simple goodness of plain, salted fudge. Need some crunch? Add a cup of your favorite nuts.

Yield: 36 pieces

2 cups semisweet chocolate chips

1 (14-ounce) can sweetened condensed milk

1 teaspoon vanilla extract

1 cup sweetened shredded coconut, divided

Dash of coarse sea salt

Melt chocolate chips and condensed milk in the microwave at 50-percent power in 20-second intervals or in a double boiler over medium-low heat, stirring constantly until fully melted and combined. Remove from heat and stir in vanilla and ½ cup coconut. Pour into a greased 9 x 9-inch baking dish and sprinkle with remaining coconut and sea salt. Allow to cool. Cut into squares for serving.

Salted Dark Chocolate Cashew Bark

Bark is one of the easiest chocolate snacks to make. Just melt chocolate and pour it onto wax paper to cool. You can add anything you like to this dark chocolate bark, but salted cashews offer the perfect flavor balance. Other tasty add-ins include pretzel pieces, potato chip crumble, and dried cranberries.

Yield: 10 servings

1½ cups dark chocolate chips

½ cup roasted, salted cashews

1 teaspoon coarse sea salt

Melt chocolate chips in the microwave at 50-percent power in 20-second intervals or in a double boiler over medium-low heat. Remove when almost melted and stir until smooth. Pour chocolate onto a wax paper-lined baking sheet, creating a ¼-inch-thick puddle. Sprinkle cashews over melted chocolate. Press down gently to partially submerge the cashews in the fudge. Sprinkle evenly with sea salt. Refrigerate for 20 to 30 minutes or until chocolate bark is firm.

Spicy Hot Chocolate

Your regular hot chocolate can't hold a candle to this spicy-sweet version that leaves you full and satisfied. Serve it steaming hot when you're in the mood for a liquid snack and enjoy the gentle heat that comes from both the warm milk and the cayenne pepper. This powdered mix keeps on giving when you save whatever you don't use in a lidded container for the next time the craving strikes.

Yield: 9 servings

3½ cups sugar

2¼ cups unsweetened cocoa powder

2 teaspoons ground cinnamon

1 teaspoon salt

½ teaspoon cayenne pepper, plus more for sprinkling

1 cup milk (per serving)

Whipped cream for topping

Whisk together dry ingredients to make the hot chocolate mix. Add 2 tablespoons of mix to a mug of 1 cup hot milk. Top with a swirl of whipped cream and sprinkle with additional cayenne pepper if desired.

Dark Chocolate Cranberry Almond Granola

If a snack category could earn an award for best sampling of many textures and flavors, granola would win. This salty-sweet granola mix brings dark chocolate together with nuts and cranberries for a natural snack that provides a mouthful of surprises with every bite.

Yield: 6 to 8 servings

2 cups old-fashioned rolled oats

1 cup walnuts, chopped

½ cup sliced almonds

½ cup roasted, salted sunflower seeds

½ teaspoon salt

2 tablespoons olive oil

3 tablespoons honey (or maple syrup)

1 cup dried cranberries

1 cup dark chocolate, broken into small pieces

Preheat the oven to 300°F. In a large bowl, stir together oats, nuts, seeds, and salt. Add olive oil and honey and toss until coated. Pour onto a greased baking sheet. Bake for 15 to 20 minutes or until golden brown. Pour into a serving bowl and allow to cool. Stir in the dried cranberries and chocolate pieces and serve.

CHAPTER FIVE

NUTTY SNACKS

Peanut Butter Swirl Brownie Bites

This kitchen classic deserves a special place in your recipe file. There's nothing that pleases a crowd more than a plate of rich, chocolate brownies swirled with creamy peanut butter and cut into bite-size pieces. With a generous sprinkle of miniature chocolate chips, these brownies are a chocolate lover's delight.

Yield: 24 servings

4 ounces unsweetened baker's chocolate

¾ cup unsalted butter

1½ cups sugar

3 eggs, lightly beaten

½ teaspoon salt

1 cup flour

¾ cup creamy peanut butter

1 cup miniature milk chocolate chips

Heat oven to 350°F. Melt chocolate pieces and butter in the microwave at 50-percent power in 20-second intervals or in a double boiler on medium-low heat and mix until combined. Mix in sugar, eggs, salt, and flour (a little at a time). Pour into a greased 13 x 9-inch baking pan. Drop spoonfuls of peanut butter into brownie batter and swirl gently with a spatula. Bake 20 minutes or until a toothpick comes out clean. Sprinkle on miniature chocolate chips and bake for another 5 minutes. Allow to cool, cut into small squares, and serve.

Cherry Pistachio Scones

Baked goods make fantastic treats when done right, especially when they include a variety of flavors and add-ins like nuts. These Cherry Pistachio Scones introduce pistachio nuts to the traditional fruit scone recipe. The results are an extra dose of texture and flavor and a robust tea-time snack.

Yield: 16 scones

2 cups all-purpose flour

2 tablespoons sugar

3 teaspoons baking powder

½ teaspoon baking soda

½ teaspoon salt

½ cup unsalted butter

¾ cup buttermilk

½ cup dried cherries

½ cup shelled, salted pistachios, chopped

Preheat oven to 400°F. In a large bowl, whisk together flour, sugar, baking powder, baking soda, and salt. With a pastry blender or fork, cut in butter until mixture resembles coarse crumbs. Stir in buttermilk. Fold in cherries and pistachios. Divide dough into 2 rounds and place on a greased cookie sheet. Bake 20 to 25 minutes or until golden brown. Allow to cool. Cut into wedges and serve.

Pecan Pralines

Pecan pralines are the perfect sweet and crunchy nut snack. More candy than cookie, these golden nuggets are little more than a collection of nuts and a blanket of rich sugar coating. It only takes six ingredients to create these delicious pralines, so they're an easy last-minute confection.

Yield: 20 pralines

2½ cups sugar

½ cup evaporated milk

½ cup salted butter

½ cup corn syrup

1 teaspoon vanilla extract

2½ cups chopped pecans

In a heavy saucepan over medium-high heat, mix together sugar, evaporated milk, butter, and corn syrup until fully combined. Bring to a gentle boil, then remove from heat. Stir in vanilla and chopped pecans. Continue to stir until mixture cools and thickens, about 5 minutes. Drop spoonfuls of pecan mixture onto baking sheets lined with wax paper. Let harden completely before serving.

Honey-Almond Bars

These salty-sweet nut bars are just the thing when you're craving a change from the norm. Forget that stale granola bar you have stashed away in your desk drawer; it's time for some serious snacking. With a blend of almonds and sesame seeds floating in a solid base of golden honey, these bars aim to please. And they will!

Yield: 8 servings

2 cups brown sugar

1 cup honey

¼ cup water

¼ teaspoon salt

¼ cup unsalted butter

1 cup roasted, salted almonds

2 tablespoons sesame seeds, toasted

In a large saucepan over medium-high heat, combine brown sugar, honey, water, and salt. Bring to a rolling boil, stirring to prevent burning. Add butter and cook for an additional few minutes. Stir in almonds and sesame seeds and remove from heat. Allow to cool slightly. Pour onto a wax paper–lined baking sheet or a lined loaf pan (for thicker bark) and allow to cool completely. Break into pieces or cut into bars and serve.

Chocolate-Covered Peanut Butter Pretzel Balls

These adorable, chocolate-covered snack balls add a dose of fun to any occasion. With a decadent peanut butter pretzel filling, these bite-size party treats are addictive enough that you might not want to share them.

Yield: 20 balls

½ cup salted pretzel pieces

½ cup creamy peanut butter

¼ cup salted butter, softened

1 cup confectioners' sugar

1 cup semisweet chocolate chips

In a food processor, process pretzel pieces until they are the consistency of breadcrumbs. In a large mixing bowl, mix together peanut butter and butter until fully combined. Gradually stir in confectioners' sugar and ground pretzels. Roll clumps of dough into 1-inch balls. Place on wax paper–lined baking sheet in freezer for 20 minutes or until firm. Melt chocolate chips in the microwave at 50-percent power in 20-second intervals or in a double boiler over medium-low heat and stir when chips are almost completely melted. With tongs, dip peanut butter pretzel balls into melted chocolate until fully submerged. Allow chocolate coating to cool and set before serving. Keep refrigerated or frozen.

Salted Almond Brittle

This simple nut brittle recipe is the quickest way to turn your favorite salted nut into a delightfully salty-sweet, handheld snack. The best parts of this snack are the crunch and the taste, but it's also a beautiful treat to display at your next party or gathering.

Yield: 4 to 6 servings

1 cup water

2 cups sugar

¾ cup honey

⅛ teaspoon salt

1 tablespoon unsalted butter

2 cups whole salted almonds

In a large saucepan over high heat, mix together water, sugar, honey, and salt until sugar dissolves completely. Bring to a boil and cook for 5 to 10 additional minutes, stirring to keep liquid from crystallizing while allowing liquid to thicken. Remove from heat and gently stir in butter and almonds until coated. Pour candied almonds into a wax paper–lined 9 x 9-inch baking pan and allow to cool and harden. Break into pieces and serve.

Hot & Spicy
Cinnamon Nut Mix

When you want to give a plain old bowl of salted mixed nuts a makeover, try adding a few of your favorite comfort-food spices along with a dash of heat. These crunchy, sugar-coated morsels are easy to make on the stove and good enough that you'll pop them in your mouth like candy.

Yield: 4 to 6 servings

¼ cup water

1 cup brown sugar

1 tablespoon cinnamon, plus additional for sprinkling

½ teaspoon cayenne pepper

3 cups roasted, salted mixed nuts

In a large saucepan over medium-high heat, mix water, brown sugar, cinnamon, and cayenne pepper. Add mixed nuts, bring to a boil, and continue to stir constantly while cooking 5 to 10 minutes or until sugar crystallizes and then smooths out after mixing. Remove from heat, break apart nuts, and cool on wax paper–lined baking sheet. Sprinkle with an extra dusting of cinnamon and serve.

Cranberry Nut Cheese Balls

These miniature cheese balls are simple to make and easy to store in the refrigerator for an impromptu snack session. Rosemary crackers are an ideal pairing for these cheese balls, but just about any cracker will complement this harmonious combination of flavors.

Yield: 8 servings

1 (8-ounce) container cream cheese, softened

1 cup feta or goat cheese

½ cup dried cranberries, chopped

½ cup pecans, chopped

½ cup chopped fresh parsley

In a small bowl, combine cream cheese and feta (or goat) cheese. Shape cheese mixture into 2-inch balls and place in refrigerator until firm. In a large, shallow dish, combine cranberries, pecans, and parsley. Roll chilled cheese balls in mixture until coated. Wrap in plastic wrap and chill in refrigerator until ready to serve.

Caramel Fudge
Peanut Bars

These delightfully fudgy snack bars get most of their crunch from whole salted peanuts and their sweetness from the golden layer of caramel topped with creamy chocolate fudge. For a faster variation of this recipe, use a jar of caramel topping in place of the homemade caramel made on the stovetop.

Yield: 12 servings

1½ cups salted peanuts, divided

1 (14-ounce) can sweetened condensed milk

½ cup dark brown sugar

6 tablespoons unsalted butter

2 tablespoons dark corn syrup

1 teaspoon vanilla extract

Dash of salt

8 ounces semisweet chocolate chips

3 tablespoons heavy cream

In a 9 x 9-inch baking dish lined with wax paper, arrange half the peanuts in a single, scattered layer. Meanwhile, in a large saucepan over medium heat, whisk together sweetened condensed milk, brown sugar, butter, corn syrup, vanilla, and salt. Continue to whisk until the sugar dissolves. Bring to a boil, stirring for a few more minutes until mixture thickens. Remove caramel from heat and pour over the peanuts in the baking dish. Melt chocolate chips and cream in the microwave at 50-percent power in 20-second intervals or in a double boiler over medium-low heat. Remove and stir when chocolate chips are almost melted. Pour chocolate over caramel layer. Sprinkle with remaining peanuts. Refrigerate until firm, cut into bars, and serve.

Index

Photo Credits

Photography by Allan Penn, unless otherwise noted below:

Page 8: © bhofack2/iStockphoto.com; 10, 11: © Magone/iStockphoto.com; 12: © Kelly Cline/iStockphoto.com; 15: © Family Business/Shutterstock.com; 16: © Ekaterina Smirnova/Shutterstock.com; 19: © Julia Sudnitskaya/Shutterstock.com; 20: © arinahabich/iStockphoto.com; 23: © Marina Shanti/Shutterstock.com; 24: © Natasha Breen/Shutterstock.com; 27: © Laura Flugga/iStockphoto.com; 28: © zi3000/Shutterstock.com; 31: © kiv_ph/Shutterstock.com; 32, 33, 37, 42, 45, 46, 73, 86, 114: © Brent Hofacker/Shutterstock.com; 34: © FabioBalbi/Shutterstock.com; 38: © Stepanek Photography/Shutterstock.com; 41: © stock-creations/Shutterstock.com; 49: © Elena Shashkina/Shutterstock.com; 50: © Josie Grant/Shutterstock.com; 53: © Christian Jung/Shutterstock.com; 54: © johnnyplease/Shutterstock.com; 57: © leungchopan/Shutterstock.com; 58: © Lena Ivanova/Shutterstock.com; 61: © Anna Hoychuk/Shutterstock.com; 63: © iravgustin/Shutterstock.com; 64, 65: © tanjichica7/iStockphoto.com; 69: © Robyn Mackenzie/Shutterstock.com; 78: © Tunedin by Westend61/Shutterstock.com; 81: © vanillaechoes/Shutterstock.com; 83: © Lauri Patterson/iStockphoto.com; 84, 85: © fcafotodigital/iStockphoto.com; 87: © hanabiyori/Shutterstock.com; 89: © TheCrimsonMonkey/iStockphoto.com; 90: © Saharose40/Shutterstock.com; 94: © Arina P Habich/Shutterstock.com; 97: © fredredhat/Shutterstock.com; 98, 102: © Elena Veselova/Shutterstock.com; 100, 101, 109: © margouillatphotos/iStockphoto.com; 105: © istetiana/Shutterstock.com; 106: © Nicoleta Raftu/Shutterstock.com; 110: © Erika Follansbee/Shutterstock.com: 113: © kuvona/Shutterstock.com; 115: © Shebeko/Shutterstock.com; 117: © Stephanie Frey/Shutterstock.com; 118: © MShev/Shutterstock.com; 120: © topotishka/Shutterstock.com

Front Cover: © Lauri Patterson/iStockphoto.com; © Arina P Habic/Shutterstock.com; © urfinguss/iStockphoto.com; © BW Folsum/Shutterstock.com; © bhofack2/iStockphoto.com; © NightAndDayImages/iStockphoto.com
Spine: © Spauln/iStockphoto.com
Back Cover: © johnnyplease/Shutterstock.com; © Kelly Cline/iStockphoto.com